U.S. DEFENSE STRATEGY AFTER SADDAM

Michael E. O'Hanlon

July 2005

FOREWORD

This paper, by Michael O'Hanlon of the Brookings Institution, reconstitutes SSI's Letort Papers series. This group of publications include papers, retrospectives, speeches or essays of interest to the defense academic community that may not correspond with our mainstream policy-oriented publications.

In this Letort Paper, Dr. O'Hanlon suggests how reductions in various weapons modernization programs and other economies might release funds for the critical needs of U.S. ground forces.

DOUGLAS C. LOVELACE, JR.
Director
Strategic Studies Institute

BIOGRAPHICAL SKETCH OF THE AUTHOR

MICHAEL E. O'HANLON is a senior fellow in Foreign Policy Studies at the Brookings Institution. His recent books include (Brookings, 2005, with Michael A. Levi), (Brookings, 2004), and (McGraw Hill, 2003, with Mike Mochizuki).

SUMMARY

In this defense strategy and budget monograph, Michael O'Hanlon argues that America's large defense budget cannot be pared realistically in the years ahead. But given the extreme demands of the Iraq mission, particularly on the U.S. Army and Marine Corps, he suggests how reductions in various weapons modernization programs and other economies might free up enough funds to add at least 40,000 more ground troops to today's military. O'Hanlon also addresses the important question of how the United States might encourage and help other countries to share more of the global military burden. Finally, he sketches other cost cutting measures such as privatization. These cost saving ideas all require serious consideration because of the enormous strain being placed on the size and cost of the U.S. ground forces.

U.S. DEFENSE STRATEGY AFTER SADDAM

What military will the United States need in the future, and how much will it cost? In an era of apocalyptic terror, and at a time of $400 billion defense budgets and $400 billion federal budget deficits, these questions are of central concern to Americans—both on national security grounds and economic grounds.

Answering these questions is extremely difficult because the United States simply does not know what type of world it will find in the future. The United States can, for the foreseeable future, be confident that its armed forces will remain engaged in Iraq, as well as in Afghanistan and other theaters related to the war on terror. It will also need to remain involved in deterrence missions in the Western Pacific, most notably in regard to Korea and the Taiwan Strait. It will wish to remain strongly engaged in European security, less because of threats to that region than because it is the continent where most of America's main security partners are located—meaning that the strength and capabilities and cohesion of the NATO alliance have important implications for the United States globally.

But the United States does not know which, if any, major new wars it may have to wage in the coming years. It does not know if relations with the People's Republic of China will continue to improve or again worsen, even risking the possibility of war over Taiwan. It does not know if the current nuclear crisis with North Korea will be resolved peacefully; it cannot predict whether any other countries will allow their territories to be used by terrorist organizations bent on attacking the United States. Additional military scenarios could be immensely important to America as well, even if they are not of the classic variety—such as civil conflict within nuclear-armed Pakistan or another between that country and nuclear-armed India, both of which could lead to large-scale stabilization or peacekeeping missions. Other major uncertainties include the degree to which the proliferation of dangerous nuclear and biological technologies can be contained, and the degree to which Islamic fundamentalism will affect the politics of countries such as Iran and Saudi Arabia in the coming years.

Thus defense planning must be based on subjective assumptions. The important thing is to postulate circumstances that are realistic but not imprudently optimistic. The nation should spend what is required on the military, including a margin of safety. But it should not and cannot waste money on its armed forces. Federal deficits are on course to remain over $400 billion and exceed $500 billion a year by the decade's end. Even if Mr. Bush is successful in halving them by then, an unlikely proposition, they are likely to grow quickly thereafter. They will thus remain at the economically unhealthy level of nearly 4 percent of gross domestic product (GDP), driving down national savings rates and increasing America's dependence on foreign investors to propel its economy. Longer-term fiscal trends are even worse, given the pending retirement of the baby boomers, together with rising health care costs.[1] The United States cannot afford to waste funds on combat formations and weapons that are not truly needed.[2]

It is easy for defense planners to dwell on the problems, but a great deal is good in today's global security situation. The United States leads a remarkable and historic alliance system. Never before has a great power elicited such support from the world's other powers and provoked so little direct opposition. These observations remain true, if more precariously so, even after the Bush administration's internationally unpopular decision to go to war against Saddam Hussein in 2003. Even powers outside this alliance system—Russia, China, India, Indonesia—generally choose to cooperate with the United States and its allies on many security issues. They are likely to continue doing so, provided that American military power remains credible, and that the U.S.-led alliance system continues to be founded (however imperfectly) on common values on which most countries agree. This conclusion can be jeopardized—by a United States that seems too unilateralist, or by allies that seem to prefer free riding to doing their fair share in international security. But what is most impressive about the western alliance system is how strong and durable it has become.

Some fear American power, and even many Americans think it is excessive. Indeed, it is impressive. But as Barry Posen convincingly argues, the United States is far from omnipotent. Past historical eras such as those during which the European colonial powers could easily conquer distant lands are gone.[3] In today's world, the United States can be understood in Posen's phrase to possess impressive command of the commons—air, oceans, and space—but to have a great deal of trouble contending with many conflicts on land, particularly against irregular resistance fighters.[4] Moreover, America's high sensitivity to casualties limits its inclination to use military force. And its highly open and democratic political system suggests that it need not be feared to the extent many do.[5]

So American power is, even in these politically contentious times, generally a force for good in the world. Alas, maintaining global military capabilities, holding together this alliance network, and preserving stability in the global system cost money. The United States presently accounts for almost half of all global military spending. But even so, the central budgetary argument of this monograph is that the U.S. defense budget must continue to rise at the pace planned by the Bush administration—roughly $10 billion a year, or 2 to 3 percent, above and beyond the inflation rate. Indeed, more funds are needed to increase the size of the active ground forces by some 40,000 personnel for several years, meaning that certain weapons programs preferred by the administration will need to be slowed or streamlined to stay within projected budgets. Once the Iraq mission is concluded, it may be possible to then hold real-dollar defense spending steady—but right now it is simply too soon to say.

U.S. MILITARY BASICS

The current U.S. defense establishment is not large in terms of personnel. U.S. troops and most types of military force structure have declined about one-third since the latter Cold War years. (They now number 1.4 million active duty troops, plus about one million reservists, of whom some 150,000 to 200,000 have been activated at any time in recent years.[6]) That active duty force is just over half the size of China's military, and not that much larger than the armed forces of India, Russia, or North Korea. Nevertheless, the American armed forces are extensively engaged around the world—not even counting the large forces now in and around Iraq. The United States has a larger military presence outside its borders than does any other country—some 400,000 troops as of early-to-mid-2005.

Republicans and Democrats generally agree about the broad contours of American military planning and sizing. Secretary of Defense Donald Rumsfeld's 2001
reaffirmed the active duty troop levels of about 1.4 million maintained during the Clinton administration and also retained most of President Clinton's agenda for weapons modernization. After September 11, 2001, Secretary Rumsfeld sought and received a great deal more budget authority than President Clinton's defense plan called for. But a Democratic president would almost certainly also have boosted defense spending after the tragic attacks, since the existing Pentagon plan was underfunded. Moreover, no major Democratic candidate for President in 2004 made a major issue out of the enormous size of the U.S. defense budget.

That Rumsfeld retained most Clinton-era ideas and programs is relatively unsurprising. Although decisions to buy specific weapons can be debated, the military needs many new or refurbished planes, ships, and ground vehicles since much of the weaponry bought during the Reagan buildup is wearing out. America's technological edge in combat may not require every weapon now in development or production, but the advantages to maintaining a resounding superiority in weaponry are evidenced in the rapid victories and relatively low casualties (on all sides, America's and its enemies') in Bosnia, Kosovo, Afghanistan, and Iraq. Talk of cutting back on ground forces during the early Rumsfeld tenure has stopped—at least for the foreseeable future—given the challenges posed by the post-Saddam Iraq stabilization mission.

The Two-War Framework and Beyond.

Since the Cold War ended, U.S. armed forces have been designed to be able to fight two full-scale wars at once. Rumsfeld modified the requirement in 2001 so that only one of the victories needed to be immediate and overwhelming.

But the basic logic of the idea was retained—and should be retained, even assuming the successful stabilization of post-Saddam Iraq. A two-war capability of some sort permits the United States to fight one war without letting down its guard everywhere else, which would undercut deterrence and perhaps increase the likelihood of a second conflict. This capability is needed with or without the Bush administration's preemption doctrine—a controversial cornerstone on which to base American security policy, but hardly a controversial concept since no U.S. president should be expected to stand by while an enemy visibly prepares an attack on this country.[7] Moreover, as Rumsfeld noted in his revised plan, the U.S. military must be able to conduct a limited number of lesser contingencies.[8]

Readiness.

There is little doubt that the readiness of U.S. military forces should be very high. That term, according to the Pentagon, refers to the ability of individual military units to perform the tasks they have been assigned in a timely and proficient way. In other words, readiness does not refer to broad choices about sizing or modernizing the military or properly defining its strategy. Instead, once these broad strategic choices are made, readiness refers to how well the DoD's individual fighting units can carry out the missions they have been assigned.

Viewed this way, readiness is still a very broad subject. Measuring it accurately requires a wide array of metrics ranging from the competence and training, and even the morale of people, to the availability of spare parts and ammunition and fuel, to the condition of major equipment. Weaknesses have arisen in readiness in certain parts of the force over the past decade, such as insufficient numbers of pilots and other technically skilled individuals and some deterioration in the availability of Air Force transport and combat aircraft. Still, readiness has, overall, been quite robust in the modern era and remains that way, though that conclusion must be tempered by the fact that DoD was far less forthcoming with readiness data recently than in the past. It may have suffered some degradation due to the high pace of recent activities, and lately was described by Joint Chiefs of Staff Chairman General Richard Myers as "good" rather than the more customary "high" or "excellent." Some indicators are worrisome, such as the increase in the rate of serious aircraft accidents.[9] But it is no surprise, and generally presents only modest risk, that recently deployed divisions or air wings or carrier groups require a few weeks or months of recovery after being deployed. So some perspective is in order. Moreover, the peculiarities of the service's readiness scoring systems, and the opaqueness of some readiness methodologies, should not be forgotten.[10] As Richard Betts reminds us, in readiness debates statistics often lie even more than they do in other spheres.[11]

Current Deployments.

Prior to September 11, 2001, the U.S. military had about 250,000 uniformed personnel stationed or deployed overseas at any given time. Just over half were in permanent bases; the others on temporary assignments away from home base and families. In broad terms, just under 100,000 U.S. troops were in East Asia (mostly in Japan and South Korea or on ships in the western Pacific), just over 100,000 were in Europe (mostly in Germany, with other substantial totals in the United Kingdom and Italy), and some 25,000 were ashore or afloat in the Persian Gulf region.

Since that time, of course, deployments have increased enormously in the Central Command's (CENTCOM) theater of responsibility, encompassing, as it does, Afghanistan and environs, as well as Iraq. As of early 2004, more than 200,000 personnel were in the CENTCOM zone (modest numbers being Coast Guard personnel or civilians working for DoD). That number included 114,000 in Iraq and 26,000 in Kuwait. All together, these deployments made for a grand total of about 400,000 uniformed personnel overseas in one place or another.[12]

DoD is planning major changes in its overseas basing.[13] Among the proposed changes are to relocate many American forces in Korea south of the Han River and out of Seoul, and to move large numbers of troops who have been garrisoned in Germany either back home or to smaller, less permanent bases in eastern Europe where they would be closer to potential combat zones.

THE PENTAGON BUDGET

America's defense budget is staggeringly high. Depending on how one estimates the spending of countries such as China and

Russia, U.S. defense spending almost equals that of the rest of the world combined. In 2002, prior to additional U.S. budget increases as well as the added costs of the war in Iraq, American defense spending equaled that of all the rest of the North Atlantic Treaty Organization (NATO), Russia, China, and Japan, combined.

That said, judging whether U.S. defense spending is high or low depends on the measure. Compared with other countries, it is obviously enormous (see Table 1 on international comparisons). Relative to the size of the American economy, by contrast, it remains modest by modern historical standards at about 4 percent of GDP (half of typical Cold War levels, though nearly twice the current average of most of its major allies). Compared with Cold War norms, it is high in inflation-adjusted or constant dollars, though not astronomically so.

The reasons for a very large U.S. defense budget are not hard to understand. The United States has security alliances or close partnerships with more than 70 overseas countries (all of the other 25 members of NATO, all of the Rio Pact countries in Latin America, several allies in the Western Pacific, and roughly a dozen countries in the Persian Gulf/Mideast region). It alone among the world's powers takes seriously the need to project substantial amounts of military power quickly over great distances for sustained periods.

Indeed, the United States possesses more than two-thirds of the world's collective power projection capability (and an even higher percentage if one focuses on high-quality units).[14] The United States alone undergirds a collective security system in the western world that helps countries from South Korea and Japan, to Kuwait and Saudi Arabia, to many NATO members, feel secure enough that they do not have to engage in arms races with neighbors, launch preemptive wars of their own, or develop nuclear weapons.

The Recent Growth in the U.S. Defense Budget.

Still, one might ask why an active duty military of the same size as the Clinton administration's has grown in cost by more $100 billion a year during the Bush presidency. Specifically, the 2000 budget for national security (DoD plus nuclear weapons activities

YEAR OR PERIOD	MEAN SPENDING LEVEL	MEAN SPENDING, Percent OF GDP
1960s (1962-1969)	382	10.7
Peak year 1968	463	9.5
1970s	315	5.9
Peak year 1970	414	8.1
1980s	379	5.8
Peak year 1989	440	5.6
1990s	359	4.1
Peak year 1991	430	5.4
2000	325	3.0
2001	328	3.0
2002	364	3.4
2003	412	3.7
2004	454	3.9
2005	445	3.7
2006	413	3.4
2007	416	3.4
2008	426	3.3
2009	436	3.3

Note: Peak years refer to the year when the inflation-adjusted dollar total was highest for the time period in question. This table shows budget function 050, including DoD and DoE (but it does not include homeland security activities except those carried out by DoD).

Source: President George W. Bush,
, Washington, DC: Office of Management and Budget, 2004, pp. 126-128.

Table 1. U.S. National Security Spending in Modern Historical Perspective (Outlays in Billions of 2005 Dollars).

of the Department of Energy [DOE]) was $305 billion and the administration's 2005 request was $423 billion.[15] Inflation accounts for 10 percent of that $118 billion increase between 2000 and 2005, but that leaves roughly $100 billion in real-dollar growth. (Note that these figures do not even count the costs of military operations in Afghanistan and Iraq that have been running at more than $60 billion annually. Of the total increase, 27 percent is in military personnel accounts, 27 percent in operations and maintenance, 17 percent in procurement, 25 percent in research, development, testing, and evaluation, and about 4 percent in nuclear weapons activities.

Of these totals, the personnel increases are due primarily to more generous compensation packages (funds for activating reservists and for temporarily increasing the size of the active duty military are primarily in the supplemental bills). The operations and maintenance increases reflect the relentless upward pressure on accounts for health care, equipment maintenance, environmental cleanup, and the like, together with the Bush administration's decision to fully fund "readiness" accounts for training and equipment maintenance. The increases in acquisition funding are partly due to missile defense ($5 billion a year higher than under Clinton), and partly to Rumsfeld's "transformation" initiatives (again, about $5 billion annually). But they also reflect the necessary decision to restore funding for hardware to historic norms after a "procurement holiday" in the 1990s.

How much does the war on terror account for this increase in the defense budget? Not very much, since, as noted, most of those costs (including those for protecting American airspace through Operation NOBLE EAGLE) are funded out of supplemental appropriations bills. The Pentagon's funding for homeland security, for example, is only about $8 billion, made up of activities such as the support provided by some 25,000 soldiers in the United States to protecting the homeland.[16] Similar activities overseas make the total for activities such as base security funded through the regular DoD budget about $10 billion annually.[17] Roughly another $5 billion may have been devoted to expansions in the classified $40 billion annual intelligence budget (hidden within DoD's budget), some of which are clearly tied to the war on terror.[18] Similarly, the annual budget for special operations command has been increased by about $3 billion, to $6.6 billion (and personnel totals by about 5,000).[19] But even adding up all these pieces, less than 20 percent of the $100 billion real-dollar growth in the annual Pentagon budget is due to the direct effects of the war on terror.

Further Planned Budget Increases.

The current era of increasing defense spending does not yet appear to be over. Expectations are for continued annual increases of about $20 billion a year—roughly twice what is needed to compensate for the effects of inflation (or to put it differently, real budgets are expected to keep rising at about $10 billion a year). By 2009, the annual national security budget would total about $500 billion, in rough numbers—about $450 billion when expressed in 2005 dollars. Indeed, given the administration's plans, that is a conservative estimate of what its future defense program would cost the country (not even including any added costs from future military operations or the ongoing missions in Iraq and Afghanistan). The Congressional Budget Office estimates that, to fully fund the Pentagon's current plans, average annual costs from 2010 through 2020 would exceed $480 billion (in 2005 dollars) and perhaps as much as $530 billion.[20]

WHAT CAN BE DONE TO CONSTRAIN FUTURE DEFENSE BUDGETS?

Given the country's security needs, it is important to spend as much on the military as is necessary. But given its fiscal predicament, it is important not to spend more than prudence dictates.

To get a rough sense of what economies may be feasible within the Pentagon budget, it is worth noting that several factors push defense spending up faster than that 1 percent real growth level—but also several may permit slower (or even zero) growth. Starting with these factors in mind makes it easier to see why 1 percent real growth is probably the right general frame of reference within which to project future defense spending.

Historically, real operating costs per uniformed individual have increased at 2 percent to 3 percent per year. Weapons costs have grown comparably. Rising health care, environmental cleanup, and other such activities affect the military as much as any other sector of the economy. For example, DoD's medical costs almost doubled in real terms between 1988 and 2003, to just under $30 billion.[21] In addition, while military compensation is now rather good for most troops (by comparison with civilian jobs requiring comparable experience and education), it is important that it stay that way. To attract top-notch people, military pay increases must keep up with civilian pay, which can require real growth of at least 1 percent a year.[22] Moreover, further increases in pay for certain specific groups may be appropriate, such as highly-skilled technicians with much more remunerative job opportunities in the private sector, or those reservists called up to active duty for extended periods who sacrifice large amounts of income as a result.[23]

Several other areas offer some hope of savings. Greater use of relatively inexpensive high technology computers and electronics can allow rapid improvements in military capabilities at modest cost. Defense efficiencies through privatization and other reforms may save at least modest sums. And greater assistance from allies may reduce overall demands on American forces, especially over a 10-year period like that being considered here.

More Burdensharing?

Today the United States outspends its major allies by about 2 to 1, but outdistances them in military force that can be projected overseas and sustained there by a ratio of at least 5 to 1. Most American allies spent the Cold War preparing to defend their own or nearby territories against a Soviet threat. American forces focused on how to deploy and operate forces many thousands of miles from home. Most U.S. allies have gotten serious about this effort only since the Cold War ended (if then).

Shifting defense responsibilities to our allies is an idea that is attractive in the United States. Unfortunately, near-term prospects for doing so to any significant degree are not good, even though many U.S. allies have good militaries, strong military traditions, and a high-tech industrial base. The problem is largely political. It is not that Europeans are as force-averse as some argue. The phrase that "Americans are from Mars, Europeans from Venus," meaning that the former are inclined to use force and the latter to use more peaceful inducements in their foreign policy, is overstated as evidenced by European military action in Bosnia, Kosovo, Afghanistan, and, to some extent, even Iraq. However, it is probably true that Europeans do not believe the world to be quite as dangerous a place as Americans typically do. And even if Europeans are far from pacifist, on average they are not quite as inclined to use force as is the United States. Several European countries face fiscal deficits that, combined with their political priorities and their voters' threat perceptions, probably preclude big defense buildups. They also have strong incentives to free-ride on U.S. commitments. European nations also often cite their substantial contributions to peacekeeping missions as evidence that they are already bearing a considerable share of the defense burden. Germany and Japan are disinclined to remilitarize, and their former adversaries, including Americans, who remember World War II, hesitate to urge them to abandon this reticence.[24]

Some progress has been made. European defense budgets have gone up about 25 percent in this decade. Their militaries are developing the combined capacity to deploy up to 60,000 troops at a considerable geographic distance and to sustain them there for a year. Japan is slowly enlarging its interpretation of which military missions are consistent with its post-World War II constitution. U.S., British, and French programs are slowly helping African militaries improve their skills. And the transatlantic quarrel over Iraq may help motivate European countries to develop more military capability to gain greater influence in decisions on the use of force. Reallocations of about 10 percent of current major allied military spending could in theory give other Organization for Economic Cooperation and Development (OECD) countries fully half as much deployable military capability as the United States within a decade.[25] That, in turn, could allow modest reductions in American troop strength, if not right away, then eventually.

Emphasizing Advanced Electronics and Computers in Defense Modernization.

One reason the Pentagon budget is slated to grow so much in coming years—with real increases of closer to 2 percent a year than the 1 percent targeted here—has to do with buying weaponry. Some of the upward pressure arises from high-profile issues such as missile defense. But most comes from the main combat systems of the military services, which are generally wearing out. Living off the fruits of the Reagan military buildup, the Clinton administration spent an average of $50 billion a year on equipment, only about 15 percent of the defense budget in contrast to a historical norm of about 25 percent. This "procurement holiday" must end, and is ending.

But the Pentagon's weapons-modernization plan is excessive. Despite Bush's presidential election campaign promise to "skip a generation" of weaponry, his Pentagon has canceled only three major weapon systems—the Navy's lower-altitude missile defense program, the Army's Crusader howitzer (which was not even particularly expensive), and more recently the Army's Comanche helicopter. Although procurement budgets must continue rising, the rapid increases envisioned in current plans are not essential. Economies can almost certainly be found through expanded applications of modestly priced technologies, such as the precision weapons and communications systems used so effectively in Afghanistan and Iraq.

The Bush plan lacks clear priorities. It proposes to replace major combat systems throughout the force structure with systems typically costing twice as much. Even though procurement budgets have not yet risen dramatically, the current plan will soon oblige them to do so—and it has already led to historic increases in the research, development, test and evaluation (RDT&E) budget for advanced systems development.[26] A more discriminating and economy-minded modernization strategy would equip only part—not all—of the armed forces with the most sophisticated and expensive weaponry. That high-end component would hedge against new exigencies, such as an unexpectedly rapid modernizing of the Chinese military. The rest of the military establishment would be equipped primarily with relatively inexpensive upgrades of existing weaponry, including better sensors, munitions, computers, and communications systems. Such an approach would not keep the procurement budget in the range of $70 billion to $75 billion, but it might hold it to $80 billion to $90 billion a year, instead of $100 billion or more. The Bush administration's 2006 budget request moved somewhat in this direction, with the announcement of plans to scale back weapons purchases for systems such as the F-22, C-130J, missile defense, and aircraft carrier fleet. But a pruning knife might still be taken to the Joint Strike Fighter (JSF), the Army's future combat systems (FCS) program, the V-22 , and several other programs.

Privatization and Reform.

All defense planners would love to save money in the relatively low-profile parts of the Pentagon budget known as operations and maintenance. These accounts, which pay for a wide range of activities including training, overseas deployments, upkeep of equipment, military base operations, and health care costs—in short, for near-term military readiness— have been rising fast in recent years, and it will be hard to stop the upward trend.[27]

Some savings are already in the works. Congress has agreed to authorize another round of base closures in 2005.[28] Since the Cold War ended, U.S. military forces have shrunk by more than one-third, yet domestic base capacity has fallen only 20 percent. Once completed, retrenchment of base capacity will save at least $5 billion annually. Overhauling military health care services by merging the independent health plans of each military service and introducing a small copayment for military personnel and their families could save $2 billion or more per year.[29] Other savings in operations and maintenance are possible. For example, encouraging local base commanders to economize by letting them keep some of the resulting savings for their base activities could save a billion dollars a year or more within a decade.[30]

All that said, these accounts are crucial to national security and have proved tough to cap or contain. Privatization is no panacea; it takes time, sometimes raises various complicated issues about deploying civilians to wartime environments, and generally saves much less than its warmest advocates attest.[31] But if operating costs can be held to a 1 percent real rise instead of the historical norm exceeding 2 percent, a slower pace of defense budget growth may someday be within reach.

These cost-saving ideas all require serious consideration because the case for increased expenditure in one part of the defense budget—the size and cost of ground forces—also needs to be made. Enormous strain is now being imposed on U.S. Soldiers and Marines by the Iraq mission and other responsibilities. Alas, there is little prospect these strains will fade away anytime soon. The top priority for defense planners today is thus to avoid breaking the American ground forces by driving out good people who decide they are no longer willing to endure the excessive pace of deployment after deployment.

ENDNOTES

1. Peter A. Diamond and Peter R. Orszag, , Washington, DC: Brookings, 2004, pp. 27-38.

2. Alice M. Rivlin and Isabel Sawhill, eds., , Washington, DC: Brookings, 2004, pp. 5-7.

3. See Jared Diamond, , New York: W. W. Norton and Co., 1997.

4. Barry Posen, "Command of the Commons: The Military Foundation of U.S. Hegemony," , Vol. 28, No. 1, Summer 2003, pp. 5-46. For a related argument, see Michael O'Hanlon, , Washington, DC: Brookings, 2000, pp. 106-167.

5. On the importance of America's transparent system, see G. John Ikenberry, "Institutions, Strategic Restraint, and the Persistence of American Postwar Order," , Vol. 23, No. 3, Winter 1998/99, pp. 43-78.

6. Department of Defense News Release, "National Guard and Reserve Mobilized as of February 25, 2004," February 25, 2004, available at . At that time, mobilized Army reservists totaled approximately 155,000; Air Force, 18,400; Marine Corps, 5,400; Navy, 2,300; and Coast Guard, 1,600.

7. President George W. Bush, , Washington, DC: White House, September 2002, pp. 13-17. For a critique, see Michael O'Hanlon, Susan Rice, and James Steinberg, , Policy Brief No. 113, January 2003.

8. See , before the Senate Armed Services Committee, 108th Congress, February 3, 2004; and Secretary of Defense Donald H. Rumsfeld, , Washington, DC: Department of Defense, September 30, 2001.

9. Myers, , p. 24; and Adam J. Hebert, "A Plague of Accidents," , February 2004, p. 59.

10. Jason Forrester, Michael O'Hanlon, and Micah Zenko, "Measuring U.S. Military Readiness," , Vol. 7, No. 2, Spring 2001, pp. 100-101.

11. Richard K. Betts, , Washington, DC: Brookings, 1995, pp. 87-114.

12. Testimony of General John P. Abizaid, Commander, U.S. Central Command, before the Senate Committee on Armed Services, March 4, 2004, pp. 1, 7-8, available at .

13. As General Richard Myers put it, "During the FY 2004 budget cycle, Congress voiced concern over the Department's overseas basing plans. Since then, our global posture strategy has matured. We are now in the process of detailed consultation with our allies and members of Congress." See Myers, , p. 33.

14. Michael E. O'Hanlon, , Washington, DC: Brookings, 2003, pp. 56-57.

15. The total 050 budget for 2003 was $456 billion, and for 2004 it was $461 billion. But those figures include supplemental appropriations for military operations of approximately $73 billion and $65 billion, respectively, for the wars in Iraq and Afghanistan and certain homeland security emergency efforts. See House Committee on the Budget, "Fiscal Year 2004 Defense and Iraq and Afghanistan Reconstruction Emergency Supplemental Appropriations," November 5, 2003, available at ; House Resolution 1559, "Making Emergency Wartime Supplemental Appropriations for the Fiscal Year 2003," January 7, 2003, available at ; Jonathan Weisman, "Military Operations in Iraq Cost Nearly $4 Billion a Month," , July 10, 2003, p. A24; and David Firestone, "The Struggle for Iraq: Senate Sends Spending Bill for War Costs to President," , November 4, 2003, p. A11.

16. R. L. Brownlee and General Peter J. Schoomaker, , February 5, 2004, pp. 8-10.

17. Steven M. Kosiak, "Funding for Defense, Military Operations, Homeland Security, and Related Activities Since 9/11," , Washington, DC: Center for Strategic and Budgetary Assessments, January 21, 2004.

18. The estimate comes from former Central Intelligence Agency (CIA) official John MacGaffin; see James Risen, "How to Improve Domestic Intelligence," , April 18, 2004, p. WK5.

19. Testimony of General Bryan D. Brown, Commander, U.S. Special Operations Command, before the Subcommittee on Terrorism, Unconventional Threats, and Capabilities of the Committee on Armed Services of the U.S. House of Representatives, March 11, 2004, p. 8, available at ; International Institute for Strategic Studies, , London: Oxford University Press, 2003, pp. 24-25; International Institute for Strategic Studies, , London: Oxford University Press, 2000, p. 31; and Department of Defense, "Special Operations Forces Posture Statement 2000," available at .

20. Adam Talaber, , Washington, DC: Congressional Budget Office, July 2003, p. 2.

21. Allison Percy, , Washington, DC: Congressional Budget Office, 2003, pp. 1-2.

22. See Amy Belasco, , Washington, DC: Congressional Budget Office, 1997, p. 5; and Lane Pierrot, , Washington, DC: Congressional Budget Office, 2000, pp. 18-23.

23. Tom Lantos, "Military Hardship Duty: Fill the 'Pay Gap' for National Guard and Reserves," , June 10, 2003, p. 23.

24. For more on the debate about Europe versus America, see Robert Kagan, "Power and Weakness," , June 2002; and Philip H. Gordon and Jeremy Shapiro, , New York: McGraw Hill, 2004.

25. For backup on those estimates, see John E. Peters and Howard Deshong, , Santa Monica, CA: RAND, 1995; Michael O'Hanlon, "Transforming NATO: The Role of European Forces," , Vol. 39, No. 3, Autumn 1997, pp. 5–15; , Washington, DC: Congressional Budget Office, 2001.

26. Steven M. Kosiak, , Washington, DC: Center for Strategic and Budgetary Assessments, 2004, pp. 15-23.

27. Gregory T. Kiley, , Washington, Congressional Budget Office, 2001. Congressional Budget Office, , Washington, DC: Congressional Budget Office, 1997.

28. Some optimists tend to exaggerate the savings from possible base closings, however. Wayne Glass, , Washington, DC: Congressional Budget Office, 1996.

29. See Ellen Breslin-Davidson, , Washington, DC: Congressional Budget Office, 1995; Russell Beland, , Washington, DC: Congressional Budget Office, 2002.

30. Robert F. Hale, , Washington, DC: Center for Strategic and Budgetary Assessments, 2002.

31. P. W. Singer, , Ithaca, NY: Cornell University Press, 2003.

www.ingramcontent.com/pod-product-compliance
Ingram Content Group UK Ltd.
Pitfield, Milton Keynes, MK11 3LW, UK
UKHW041901190726
13854UKWH00003B/1009

9 781312 325302